The Princess and The Dragon:

A Man's Guide to Understanding Himself in Relation To His Wife

Prayer does not change God, but it changes him who prays -Soren Kierkegaard

Knights Fight, Princes Learn, Kings Rule.

The Princess and the Dragon:

A Man's Guide to Understanding Himself in Relation To His Wife

Foreword-

Now I know some of you may be thinking some interesting thoughts about the title of this book. I assure you that the title has all good intent involved. I am the wife that is often referenced in this book. Though you may have your own wife, and the rivers of who she is run deep and are rough at times, let me encourage you that the dragon you may sometimes experience is still the princess you married. I know the rivers of your own soul, as a man, run deep as well, and we have our own journey to take with learning the depths of who you are, but take heart in knowing that what you give us as wives in true understanding of the feelings we hold will come back to you in the patience and love in which you give it. I know, like my husband, you have given so much already, and at times you may feel lost in who you've become. Let me encourage you to stand strong and steadfast as a knight readied for battle. The battle will not be with us as women and wives, but it will be within you to become more vulnerable to our cries while strengthened at the onslaught of our emotions.

You can have confidence in knowing that God has properly equipped you to handle that woman in your care. You can vanquish that dragon in her and win back that princess and by doing so, inherit a love and dedication that won't quit. I still have a little dragon in me at times, but my knight has learned how to get his princess back. The dragons that may have grown in your wife may have taken a form that comes out looking like aggression, apathy, depression, overindulgence or sometimes just pure bitterness. That dragon can manifest in many different forms at different times in the course of your marriage. But trust me when I say, God has fully equipped you to take back your princess. Your weapons aren't carnal but they are capable of pulling down strongholds. You'll discover your greatest weapons against all the fire we blow at you. You'll have us blowing smoke as we yield and flourish. If we've yielded but not flourished, check your weapons. They may be forging another dragon instead of vanquishing one. I wish I could tell you that you'd never get wounded on your quest to vanquish our dragon heart, but faithful are the wounds of a friend. You'll live and thrive to fight another day. Just not every day! Now enjoy this book as my knight tells you how he has learned to tame his Princess/Dragon. (If you wanna call me tamed….*smirk*)

From a rescued princess,

Felacia

Chapter 1- Know That You're a Knight, Know That You're a King

I can distinctly remember just after I graduated high school in beautiful Aurora, Colorado. We seniors were able to stop going to campus about a week before school actually got out. Graduation is an ecstatic time, with rolling waves of emotion, and an excitement akin to riding the incline on a roller coaster, knowing you're about to rocket down the other side. I was as excited as some of the other seniors, but also apprehensive. I really dreamed of going to the University of Colorado at Boulder, and at the time, I wanted to major in Film Directing. I wanted to be the next Stephen Spielberg. Looking back now, I don't understand why I thought CU Boulder was any kind of training ground for film directors... so, you can see my immaturity. Of course, by God's Divine Providence, that dream fell through, and my next recourse was very unclear. I just knew I was going to be graduating and the ceremony was coming up soon.

At the time, I was generally aimless about who I wanted to be other than in a vague sense, so I recall driving up to the school one day, maybe an hour before school let out. I walked up the halls in a fog. My first three years were not exceptional, but by senior year, things had changed drastically. I lost about 25 pounds over the year from a combo of swimming class and P.E., and I had gotten somewhat of a name for myself as a writer and cartoonist on the school paper. I actually enjoyed that year. Had the other years been like senior year, I would have wanted to stay for a fifth year. So obviously, there were mixed emotions about leaving. All these thoughts were milling around in my mind as I wandered the vast but familiar halls, not really noticing anyone. It seemed like out of nowhere, I felt someone touch my arm. It was one of the freshmen that I knew pretty well.

"Man, what are you doing here?!," he said, his face a mixture of incredulity and shock.

"I dunno, just-just walking, looking around...", I stammered. Honestly, I was more than a little embarrassed.

"Man, if I was a senior about to graduate, I would never come back here. Didn't they let you guys out a week early?"

By this point, I really just wanted to slink back out to the car. I never forgot that feeling, a feeling of being in one place that doesn't fit you anymore, having just advanced to another. Some of us, as men, don't high step through life with determination so much as we stumble through like stone drunks, half aware of where we really are.

Marriage in the early years was like that for me. In fact, I think it was worse than those cloudy last days of high school. I stumbled through husbandry (fun fact: the word *husband* is the English word for "farmer") in the young days of our marriage, really not knowing who I was supposed to be as the man of our home. We men can say our vows, but that doesn't mean we understand what we are committing to do and to become. The knight in shining armor from those invigorating days of dating that lovely princess is now the king of his own country. We love exploring those rolling hills and the deep, wondrous valleys, but that uncharted land called the mind of a woman can be a wild, daunting adventure. God made it that way. I believe God wanted our wives to be a great unknown,

7

set for us to explore and conquer and love. Far too many of us men conquer, but as tyrants, who rape and pillage, sweeping across the land like an angry, ferocious tidal wave. And we wonder why so many women are so angry. Even though I didn't always understand the fierceness of Felacia's anger, it was never in question to me as to why she was angry. Somehow, the gentle, soft care of the knight who knows he is now the king soothes the savage beast. I knew <u>why</u> she was angry, but to her it was important that I <u>cared</u> why she was angry. I had to know who I was to be able to care. Jesus cared about other people because he knew who He was. Eleanor Roosevelt said, "Friendship with one's self is all important, because without it, one cannot be friends with anyone else in the world."

When we make the transition from bachelor to husband, it is a pivotal moment. In those moments, being a friend to yourself, knowing who you are, is so important to surviving the transition. Some transitions in life are pivotal, like womb to birth, elementary to middle school, high school to college, college to career, single to married. Our lives are full of these transitions from one title to another. And the transition into husbandry may be the greatest of all, second only to a commitment to God Himself. Like riding a boat on a raging sea, we have to have a firm grasp on the railing through the change, or we will be cast overboard.

I was cast overboard, but unlike the Apostle Peter, I did not ask Jesus if I could walk out there to Him. I was too preoccupied, too young, too dumb. I had no clue that I had made a transition. I didn't know I was a knight, and I definitely didn't know I had become a king. Becoming the king seems grand and glamorous, but it is actually a great commission. Jesus gave man a great commission to go into all the world and preach the gospel. Paul the Apostle then commissions us as men to love our wives as Christ loves the church. The hard part about loving your wife as Christ loves the church is that we men are human. Our wives are human. Our imperfections can make us hard to love. There are going to be times when you come in from work, you've had a hard day, and you're ready to unload. As soon as you walk in, she's passing the baby to you and complaining about how rough her day was. You listen to her complaints and never get around to talking about your day. Or you may come in and she's mad, and you don't know why. All you know is you're not in the mood.

These are the times when being the knight in shining armor is very hard work. It's a lot like working in whatever trade you're in. I'm a machinist by trade, and there are days when I go in to work, and the boss lines out the job for the day, and we roll our eyes in dread. We know we're about to get sweaty and greasy, probably picking up heavy compressor valves, or working out in a unit with boiling hot condensate dropping on your back while you are trying to tighten a nut that could stand to be a foot closer to you. There are easy days where everyone is sitting in the break shack, waiting on a call and watching tv. There are other days where you go home exhausted, muscles aching, and you have to be back in the morning. Sometimes being a husband can be that way. And the wife can be like your boss. "No excuses, just get it done!" Just like I have to know I'm a machinist on those hard days when I go in, I have to know I'm the knight, the king, the husband, especially during those hard times. What is the alternative on my job if I don't want to do something? I can quit or get fired. Or I can do the job.

What is your alternative if you don't want to be the husband that day?

Push her away. Ignore her. Divorce. Or be the knight. Be the king. In practical terms, listen to her. Then ask her to listen to you and let her invest in the things on your mind. Give her a task as she gives you a task. In your hard days, you can walk through together.

Chapter 2- Have the tools for the rescue

Have you ever heard a tale of a knight saving a princess from a fierce dragon in which the knight had absolutely no weapons? No sword, no shield, no armor.... nothing but good will and good intentions? I'm sure at some juncture in the history of storytelling, there was such a tale, but the reason that we are not hearing it now is because the poor rescuer DIED! One of the key elements of the knight's tale is that he succeeds because he is properly equipped for the job. Imagine this: one of the great sequences of any true '80s action movie is the montage where the hero is gearing up. We see him carrying an M-60 machine gun, and he's strapping on a bandolier full of foot-long cartridges over a scarred up, muscular chest. He sheathes his massive, razor-sharp survival knife. He pulls on and tightly cinches high black military combat boots. He doesn't need a shirt because he's bulletproof. And then the mission begins.

But so often, we, as husbands, go to the rescue of our sweet princesses completely ill-equipped and unprepared for the battle. Felacia and I are in our 19th year of marriage, but I'm a non-expert, in fact. I'm STILL learning her every day. There were probably at least seven really rough years in the beginning (She'd probably say 10!), but all 19 have been a journey almost like the journey Frodo takes in the Lord of the Rings trilogy, a journey where there are minutes or hours that feel like everything will crumble at any second, a feeling like watching the action hero's leap through a shattering window just as a building explodes in an epic show of physics. The feeling that the two of you, husband and wife, have just barely escaped something that would have destroyed the one of you, forever. Yes, I said "the one of you". The Bible, in Mark 10:8-9, says "and the two shall become one flesh. So they are no longer two but one flesh. What therefore God has joined together, let not man separate." The two become one. But how can we be one when both of us lack so much understanding of the other, and sometimes neither one knows quite what to say. Yep, definitely not an expert! But I do know THE expert, and His wisdom is what we will use to guide our journey.

Now why don't we go into the battle for the hearts and souls of our women prepared, well-suited for the task, full of righteous desire and ready to save our princesses? Put simply, we don't realize that the fierce dragon we are rescuing our princess from is often the princess herself. Yes, the princess IS the dragon. If by chance you're reading this with your wife, this may be the part where she makes you sleep on the couch, but bear with me.

The reason that your beautiful, honey-voiced, sexy woman has become that fierce, roaring, furious dragon is wrapped up in so many layers. Some of those layers have absolutely nothing to do with you! That fact may come as a blinding surprise, as it has surprised me so many times. We talked about that dark place before, you know, the dark, dripping cave that you approach with your sword drawn and your shield firmly in front of you. The place where the dragon lay, waiting. Our princesses often lie in wait for us in that dark cave, but when we first meet them, that cave is seemingly nowhere in sight. You see her as the attractive woman at work, out shopping, hanging out with her friends, at any one of the many places we stumble across our treasures while meandering through life. You ask her out, or perhaps she asks you. Dating and courtship becomes an ignorant, if temporary, bliss. Perhaps you make it down that quick chute of courtship to engagement, and it leads to your wedding day. It's after the wedding vows, during those years of getting to know each other as husband and wife, that you as a husband may gradually begin to see your princess retreating, whether quickly or ever so slowly, fading into that dark cave you knew nothing about.

The first few times it happens, we either don't seem to care or like fools, we rush in, sword swinging, eager to rescue and save the day. When we emerge from the cave, her little hand firmly in our grip, we bring her into the light and realize she's been wounded. She's got little gashes or big ones, wounds we have given from our aggressiveness as knights. The awful realization sets in, "I did that to her, but I don't understand how!"

Your heart sinks as a man. You don't understand.

"I was only trying to help", you think. Sometimes you even say it to her, and she screams, "You didn't help me, you hurt me!" Somehow, it all becomes your fault, and the grand visions of "fixing it", of saving the day, all come crashing down.

I'm sure husbands may find that their wives have different ways of sorting through very deep and real feelings that, honestly, men don't understand. I believe at some point, all wives cry. Some may drink alcohol excessively to silence their issues. Some call a trusted friend. Some fade. Some take a long, reflective walk. But all married women have times where they are in a place their husbands don't understand, or can't seem to go with them. Sometimes, directly or indirectly, husbands have led their wives into these dark places by way of: Infidelity, lack of concern, pornography, abusiveness, or control issues. There are so many things that can lead a wife to a dark and lonely place that her husband may feel he cannot follow. Many times what leads a wife into her cave has happened to her before she ever met or married her husband.

But all is not lost. Wikipedia, in its entry <u>Princess and Dragon</u> states, "When the tale is not about a dragon but a troll, giant, or ogre, the princess is often a captive rather than about to be eaten, as in The Three Princesses of Whiteland. **These princesses are often a vital source of information to their rescuers,** telling them how to perform tasks that the captor sets to them, or how to kill the monster, and when she does not know..... she frequently can pry the information from the giant. **Despite the hero's helplessness without this information, the princess is incapable of using the knowledge herself.**" I put these passages in bold because they highlight something very important. Oftentimes, Felacia had information for me that would aid in my ability to go to the sad, dark places where she would find herself as a woman, but if I was not careful, and gentle, I would neglect this valuable information in my zeal to fix things. As was stated, she had the information, but was incapable of using the knowledge herself. Yet she had the tools available right there for me to use in her rescue.

You are probably confused by your wife, perhaps desperately so, as she is taking that long drive or walk, or she's somewhere in the house avoiding you and pushing you away because you don't understand. So you ask, "What in heaven's name are the tools to vanquish the dragon and rescue the princess, and how do I get them?" I can honestly say I don't know the answer to that question because there are no formulas, but I can tell you what I have seen in regards to my marriage.

1. Listen to what your wife says

2. Care enough about what she says to find out what she really means

3. And finally, change those things that are in your power to change

All these points may seem like very abstract, very feminine ideas, so let's break them all down into simple, masculine ideas. I'll tell you a story. My day job is not really a day job. I work primarily night shift. I get off work at 4 am, come in, usually sleep until maybe 10 or 11 am. Yesterday, I worked off of my weekly shift. Felacia asked me if I wanted to go out to lunch with her. She asked, but she knows I can be grumpy about leaving the house, especially when I've been working. But she sweetly asked me because she knew I'd be hungry, and we could spend some time together before the kids got in from school. I said sure, so we went to the car. She went to the passenger's side, so I got in the driver's side. I sat down, but I was a bit annoyed. In my mind, I'm thinking "She should drive since I've been at work all night, and I just got up."(Operative word here is *thinking*.) So I crank the car and she asked me what I wanted to eat. Now my annoyance dialed up to a 10. I was a bit sharp when I said, "I don't know! I figured you had a place. I don't feel like picking anything today. I don't feel like making any decisions". I think I may have gone on complaining for the whole drive, adding my complaint about having to drive.

I'm sure many guys can identify with this scenario in one form or another. The problem in her view was not that I didn't want to drive or pick where we ate. The problem was that I didn't communicate that to her. Felacia is a very exhaustive communicator, meaning, I don't have to wonder what her opinion is about most things. I am generally quiet, and so I don't express what I want a lot of the time. This is probably a tendency I garnered from childhood. If I don't express my wants, I don't have to hear "No" as an answer. Felacia spoils me really, because she does a lot of things without me having to ask her. This allows me not to have to communicate. Many women are very detailed, even quiet-natured ones, especially when it comes to expressing their feelings. Men are often more definite in their approach and less exhaustive, but this can lead to a lack of detail from a woman's perspective. I expected her to know I didn't want to drive or pick a place to eat. She expected me to communicate that. Women can often be very definite about their feelings and wishes but that doesn't mean that they are clear about ours. We have to communicate our wants and needs to them and effectively communicate at that. Communicating with her effectively was within my power to change in this instance. This goes back to those tools for the job.

Care and concern become armor at this point. I know Felacia. I know she's a communicator. I know she's an at-home mom who is doing a wonderful job raising kids after working for 18 years as a nurse. Not feeling like she's overworking me is very important to her. I know she doesn't like to feel like she's pressuring me to do things or go places if I don't want to. I know all these things, but if I don't remember that I care about those feelings she has and that I'm concerned about how she'll take my response, I'll be walking into battle without armor. I know Felacia very well, and I know the things that make her sad. I know a lot of things that make her happy as well. However, knowing those things but not caring enough to exercise that knowledge when it counts creates the dragon. Now fellas, I'm not saying you'll get this right with your princess every time, but just keep it in mind as you interact with her.

It was so simple in hindsight. All I had to say was "Honey, can you drive us? I'll go eat wherever you choose as long as you pick where we go". Instead, that whole 45-minute car ride turned into me complaining and her breathing fire about how she felt about my reaction toward her not driving. That 45 minutes could have been spent just enjoying each other. We made the following minutes better as we talked through it but like I said in the beginning, I'm not an expert!

Guys, one burning issue that we need to address is this: we know what I should have done, or at least what may have been more effective in this situation, but why didn't I handle it that way? Why did I choose to get annoyed and frustrated instead of communicating? The fact is that married folk have history with each other, good and bad history. My thoughts at the time were: as many times as I have gotten off of night shift and got up midday to go somewhere, she should already know I don't want to drive or do any major thinking. That's my history. She should know I'm tired. Historically, when I'm tired I don't want to go anywhere. She should know I'm grouchy. She **should** know…. And that's the catch. When I'm tired or just not in the mood to have a "talk" or argue, I may avoid a potential argument. So sometimes I just hope she gets it. I found out after we talked that Felacia wasn't intentionally trying to make me drive; she was so excited about our excursion that she didn't even think about driving. Had I asked her, I believe she would have eagerly gotten in the driver's seat. I have a friend, on the other hand, whose wife was the type of woman that was willing to let him do everything as long as she didn't have to do it. That same incident would have required a discussion between him and her. He would have had to have told her "I need you to drive" and been ready to explain what he needed from her in the future. And that's the key. There may be times when as a man you need to have a discussion about your needs with your wife just as she probably has with you. Don't expect her to read your mind, and don't let yourself fall into the trap of avoidance in hopes of keeping the peace. If there is an issue between you and you're generally the one to avoid issues, be the initiator. Guilt, whether actual or perceived, can lead us not to communicate effectively. Believe it or not, you are still exercising care and concern when you enter those discussions that sometimes turn into arguments. You care enough to talk or argue through it to reach an understanding. Remember, knights not only save the day, they have to fight too.

I think we men meet our wives and are paragons of care and concern when we first meet them. Fights or arguments are the furthest thing from our minds. We want to know what's her favorite dessert. Where does she like to shop? Does she like dogs or cats? Every detail that creates the beautiful woman sitting there is fascinating. If she's allergic to cat hair and your parents have a cat, it is very important to you to let mom know to put the cat away when your lady comes to visit them for the first time. You care and you want to impress her. You're concerned about her health and well-being. You want her to know that you are thinking about her and can take care of her needs. After you marry that dream girl, that need to express care and concern is gradually replaced by "She knows I care about her". You think "I put a roof over her head", "she's got a nice car", "she doesn't want for anything...." You quit trying, quit digging, quit pursuing the princess in an effort to conquer the world. But in the midst of your pursuit of world domination, your wife wants to know that she is your world. And you'd be amazed that your passion for her can often be shown in the smallest of things. Maybe you buy her roses every week, and she's come to expect them. Mix it up for her sometimes. Do something different. Felacia likes coffee and tea. One day I unexpectedly brought home some exotic teas and some Starbucks pods for the Keurig. You'd have thought I'd bought her a diamond ring. She was so amazed and thankful! (Who knew!)

Regular acts of kindness toward your princess make her happy. Just sitting and talking to her, and actually caring about what she has to say, goes a long way. Now in all honesty, sometimes, you may not care, but believe me, act like you do and you'll be unsheathing a very effective tool. The more you use that tool called care, the more you'll learn to care. That armor of showing care and concern has rendered you impenetrable. Her fire is having no real effect on you because you're deflecting it back onto her as care and concern for her thoughts and feelings. Fighting fire with fire gets both parties burned. Douse those flames with some care and concern, and you'll begin to see that princess again.

One key element in our journey together is to realize that even as I gear this book to men, God is fully aware that your wife is not perfect. I can remember feeling so aggravated when I was trying to work on the issues I felt I had as a man and a husband and believing that Felacia's biggest issue, in my mind, was that she thought she had no issues. I felt that I was her only problem! In fact, I thought she felt she was perfect before I came along. I used to get angry at God thinking, "Why do you only put pressure on the man to change?" I can remember a saying that basically stated that Men marry women hoping that they will never change, and women marry men hoping to change them. If you feel like you are changing for the better but she doesn't see it, don't worry. God sees the areas that your wife needs to grow in. The important thing for each and every person, male or female, to realize is that you cannot change another person, you can only change yourself. Even as we seek the changes that we need to make as knights and men, rest assured that the part of the apple that Eve ate is going to be addressed as well.

Knights fight, but princes learn. Princes are learning how to rule a kingdom. You start your marriage as a knight, but instantly become a prince, learning all you can about this lady in your life, her imperfections and her strengths. It is so important in your new role not to always approach her as a knight, even in shining armor. You're a prince now. And you are learning her.

Chapter 3- It's not about you (Your love For Her)

One of my favorite scenes in the Pixar film The Incredibles is the one where Bob Paar, who is the retired superhero Mr. Incredible, has just come in really late from work. The Paar family has been put into the superhero relocation program, and no one is supposed to know they are superheroes. But Bob has been sneaking out with his other superhero buddy, Frozone, going around saving the day like they used to do in the good old days. Bob's wife Helen, AKA Elastigirl, waits up for him, upset, and she begins to question where he has been. Bob has traces of rubble on his shoulder, so he has to admit to Helen that, in performing a rescue, he and Frozone have knocked a building down.

HELEN

You know how I feel about that, Bob. Darn you! We can't blow cover again!

BOB

The building was coming down anyway.

HELEN

What?! You knocked down a building?!

BOB

It was on fire. Structurally unsound. It was coming down anyway.

HELEN

Tell me you haven't been listening to the police scanner again?

BOB

Look, I performed a public service. You act like that's a bad thing.

HELEN

It is a bad thing, Bob! Uprooting our family again, so you can relive the glory days is a very bad thing.

BOB

Reliving the glory days is better than acting like they didn't happen!

HELEN

Yes! They happened! But this, our family, is what's happening now, Bob. And you are missing this! I can't believe you don't want to go to your own son's graduation.

BOB

It's not a graduation. He's moving from the fourth grade to the fifth grade.

HELEN

It's a ceremony!

BOB

It's psychotic! They keep creating new ways to celebrate mediocrity but if someone is genuinely exceptional...

HELEN

This is not about you, Bob. This is about Dash.

BOB

You want to do something for Dash? Then let him actually compete. Let him go out for sports!

HELEN

I will not be made the enemy here! You know why we can't do that.

BOB

Because he'd be great!

HELEN

This is not about you!

The Mrs. and I have laughed and recalled that scene many times since we first watched that movie because it is so true. The life we have built together, raising our kids, working, buying, and constructing the American dream, all great and wonderful endeavors, can slowly but surely create a thick coating over married life, like a slowly clogging artery, a coating of mundane apathy. Life can become robotic. Restlessness sets in. In the pursuit of happiness, you find you're not always happy. You're not unhappy, but you're not happy either. You're just there. The passion for anything, for life itself begins to wane. The knight in shining armor has hung up his shield and started an armor polishing business, a

24

very successful one. This success allows him to rarely go out and conquer anything anymore. Did I mention that the knight has now transitioned to prince and then to King, and the princess is now his queen and she rules alongside him? They raise their children. He's comfortable. The family seems to be comfortable. But he is fading, receding into himself. He's aloof, going through the motions. And his Queen is trailing along behind him needing him to get it together. Then one day, rumors begin to surface of a dragon afoot.

The knight in him returns with a dim flame of passion that begins to grow. An adventure awaits him.

Maybe as his Queen toils away with their family, he's noticed a little, cute princess in the office. She needs rescuing too, right?

Maybe there is a treasure chest full of loot to consume him. There's money to be made! He gets wrapped up in his job.

Maybe there are princesses on flickering screens in hideaway places doing things that shouldn't be on a tv screen for all to see, and now he's hooked.

Maybe he's hiding flagons of ale inside his rusting armor so the Queen won't realize he's turning into a drunk.

Maybe it's all sorts of things, besetting sins, distractions, habits and hobbies. No matter what he's ensnared in, life has become all about him. The knight has become King David, looking over a balcony at Bathsheba bathing when he should be leading his men on the field of battle. When knights become kings, when success cools the fighting spirit, a man can become a shell of his former self, and the princess, who has become the queen, suffers as a result of his apathy. The princess turned queen begins to turn into the dragon again.

Your love for your wife is a shield. I'm not talking about a feeling here. There is something about remembering why you loved her in the first place that shields you from being wounded when she is wounded either by you or by life. You go in to vanquish a dragon and rescue a princess, only to realize that the princess has turned into the dragon you've come to slay. That shield of love protects you from the fiery blast of breath meant to incinerate you. That shield allows you to approach her without her flames burning you to a crisp before she remembers that you aren't the devil himself. For a married man, if he's not careful, the good old days were not the days when he and his princess first married. The good old days are the days before the ol' ball and chain, the days before the wife and kids, when he was the wandering knight conquering the world. The focus of a man, while a good thing, can become a bad thing. In the midst of his focus, he can lose his family. The knight can become like Bob Paar, focused on the good ol' days and the potentially great days ahead are slipping by like phantoms.

It's not about you, Sir Lancelot.

Knights fight. Princes learn. And Kings rule.

It's about us.

There was a period of time when Felacia and I were young married. A few years in, and the arguments, pressure, and conflicts seemed endless. I began to wonder what in the world I had ever seen in her. All I thought I saw was an evil witch, a fire-breathing dragon who was constantly angry at me about things I had done or things I was going to do. Of course, I also knew much of her anger was justified. I was very selfish, and quite immature for a young man in his mid-twenties. There was a lot I didn't know. I had a real problem with pornography that I had developed in college, and it was tearing us apart. I was extremely sensitive to criticism. Meanwhile, due to some things in her childhood, Felacia was very aggressive about controlling her outcomes, had a tendency to dominate conversations, and tended to see the world as more black and white than I did. It was a challenging time to say the least. I wanted to go with the flow, but as the head of household, I didn't realize that a young wife trying to follow her husband's lead would feel very fearful of following a man who had a habit of just "letting it happen". So we conflicted a lot.

It reached a point where I think we both wondered what in the world we ever saw in each other. There came a day (I don't remember the date or what I was doing) that I can recall thinking yet again, "She's always mad and whining or yelling about something. What did I ever see in her?" That sounds so harsh to me now. These days of late, I have begun to draw out the sweet princess I knew in those first days of young love. But at that time, the struggle was real! I know that the Holy Spirit, God's presence with us on earth, spoke softly to my hard, frustrated male heart. As a Believer in Christ Jesus, I know God speaks to us about everyday struggles, and in fact, I often wonder how marriages make it without Him. Anyhow, God softly spoke to my tormented mind.

"What was it about Felacia that made you choose to love her in the first place?"

I had to take a deep breath and remember. You'll notice I didn't say "fall in love". I chose to love her. She chose to love me. The single act of choosing is what enabled us to recall why we loved each other to begin with. Falling in love is just what it sounds like, an accident. The act of falling. You can't help it. So falling out of love is also an accident, a convenient one. "Oh, we just fell out of love with each other...." It's a passive way of loving someone that leaves no responsibility for choices. So when hard times come in a marriage, passive love doesn't choose to remember why you "fell" for your spouse because love just "happened". In a healthy marriage, you don't fall in love, you choose to love. So as an active participant in this great journey called marriage, I had to sit and remember what things I loved about Felacia. She's very bubbly and loves to laugh and be silly. I'm very serious, and the person she is fascinates me. She loves Jesus with all her heart. I knew if she loved Jesus, she could love me. I loved her gorgeous smile, those long legs, that ponytail swinging back and forth when she walked by. I love her intensity, her passion when she talks about things that interest her. I love to hear her sing. There were and are many things I love about Felacia, enough so that I wanted to make that life journey with her. As she has moved from the princess to the queen, new things about her continue to keep me fascinated.

Now you may be thinking, "I get you, but so far it seems like it's still all about the man". Here is where it becomes all about us. In remembering the woman you chose to love, you are creating a shield from the fiery dragon that you are trying to approach now. Imagine yourself, a knight in full armor, with a glistening shield as tall as you at your front, the flames blasting directly at it, and careening to either side of the shield, like falling water against rocks. You slowly, methodically advance, the shield protecting you, as you try to get closer and closer. Are you approaching so you can kill the dragon? I hope not! If you wanted to kill her, you'd shoot arrows from far away (which we men often do to our wives). But you're approaching this way because you want the princess to be safe. It's about her, not protecting yourself from her or from anything. It's in the approach, it's in the caring about her and the concern, that the dragon is finally calmed down, and the lady is won. A man's mind is often on getting there, but a woman's mind is often on getting there safely. It's the fact that you came to her in spite of her fire breathing that wins her heart again. It's the fact that you're there and that you care. It's not that you can fix it or that you have all the answers. Sometimes, when Felacia and I talk, it's just in the act of talking that she gets the answer she seeks. She appreciates the fact that I took the time just to talk, to take that verbal journey with her. When we were young, talking became tedious because I was always on the defensive. "Whatchu tryin' to say?!", I'm thinking. Now I find that I can weed through things so much better as we talk, and if she says something I don't agree with, I can say, "I don't agree." I remember she's my friend, not my antagonist, not an opponent in the ring of life that I have to take down. I'm not here to make her "tap-out". It's no longer all about me.

And it's such a relief.

Chapter 4- Asking for Directions

Felacia told me a story once about a trip she took with a friend in high school. They were headed from home in the mid-east part of the state of Alabama to an event in New Orleans. She was riding with her friend's older sister and her friend's mother and father. The father had gotten written directions from a friend on his job on how to get to his destination, but something got lost in translation.

Now the father had a pretty domineering personality, and he wasn't known for his kindness to say the least. His treatment of his wife colored the whole event for me as I listened to the story. As the trip progressed, the man had somehow managed to head in the complete opposite direction of his destination, and being the domineering, hard-headed man that he was, he wasn't listening to any of the admonishments from his wife and daughter about going the wrong way. He must have thought to himself, "My friend gave me directions, he knew what he was talking about, and that is the end of that!" He refused to admit that he was lost and headed in the wrong direction. Felacia told me that they drove for several hours, eventually ending up in the state opposite of the state they were headed to. She said they stopped and asked for directions several times along the way. There was even a map in the car. All the tools were there to make a complete 180 degree turn back in the right direction. Instead, they took a trip of 242 miles in the wrong direction just because the driver didn't want to admit he'd made a wrong turn. Sometimes we will keep heading in a direction we know is wrong simply because we feel like we've gone too far to stop and turn back. Remember, it's never too late to turn around and head in the right direction, especially when you know that you're heading the wrong way. I think the biggest reason for this man not changing directions was that he didn't like who this information was coming from: his wife and his daughter.

Eleanor Roosevelt once said something in relation to this issue of men and women that fascinated me. She said, "Too often the great decisions are originated and given form in bodies made up wholly of men, or so completely dominated by them that whatever of special value women have to offer is shunted aside without expression". All too often, we husbands disregard the contributions and help of our wives. The Bible calls the wife a "helpmeet", which means she is the one person on the earth truly tailored to help you make decisions, to partner with on your life goals together, and to help get you back on the right course if you start to veer off. Yet as I listened to this story, I had to acknowledge that, at more times than I would like to admit, I have been even more thickheaded than the "hero" of our story. I have been so consumed with being right, or doing something right, that I continued heading in the wrong direction just because I didn't want to admit that I was wrong. In fact, just today in talking to Felacia, I had to apologize about an insensitive act that I committed against her on our wedding day. For much of our 18 years of marriage, in my own way, I tried to make up for it, or at least show her that I realized how wrong I was to react as I did. The one thing I had never done was to look her in the eye and say to her that I was genuinely sorry, because I did not realize how much the incident hurt her.

The proverbial car was moving, but I was driving the wrong way with this particular issue. I had been driving the wrong way for years! I knew what I meant to do, where I meant for us to go, but all the while, I never stopped to ask for directions. Making up for what happened was not important to Felacia. Making up for it was important to ME. Acknowledging that it happened and how it made her feel WAS important to her. That part, trying to fix things, is what tells me that I am a good man, or at least better than the man I was then. A man can get lost in trying to be the knight and miss being

32

her true hero. Fixing it, making wrong right, is considered a duty and a challenge to a man. A knight should have a strong sense of justice and a desire to right wrongs. As true knights, one of our main goals in the relationship with our wives should not be proving to her who you are, but being who God made you to be. If you forgot your anniversary, own up to it, and any hurt it caused, without excuses, and then go enjoy it with her anyway. If you cheated on her, and by some miracle she takes you back, be willing to listen to her recollections of the incident as many times as it takes for her to find peace with it and with you. If she tells you painful things about her childhood or her past, don't try to figure out how to fix it. Just listen and try to understand how she feels about it. This is where the knight is the prince who is to become king; he is learning his wife. Once again, princes are there to learn.

Again, I say these things not as an expert, but a man striving to be my best for both of us. I fail miserably sometimes at the very things I'm recommending, yet I still have faith that I can see these changes coming to pass. God didn't give us the gift of marriage if He didn't think it could be done. As it turns out with this particular issue, the Mrs. and I were able to talk through what happened all those years ago, and I understood her viewpoint in a different way than I have understood it for 19 years. It helped me to realize I had been approaching the feelings she had been having about the incident for all those years from completely the wrong angle, and I didn't even see it. For a long time in my younger days, it was ignorance and embarrassment and stubbornness that hindered me from seeing what she saw. I hated to be wrong, and I hate to do things the wrong way. I also hated asking for help with things I didn't know or understand. I didn't think asking for help was manly. Later on, it was a lack of understanding that hindered me, and not so much my ego. I really wanted to be better, and to feel where she was coming from, so I just needed to hear it in a way I could understand. I wasn't embarrassed in our last conversation about it, I really cared far less about being wrong, and I genuinely wanted to understand how she had been feeling all those years. There is probably a lot I still don't know about all the things Felacia was thinking and feeling at the time, and there may be more that she may reveal one day, but I felt like I actually understood her in a way that I hadn't before.

I don't know about you, but when I am driving and I get lost, or I have a question about something that I have always wondered about, finding the right path or finding the answer is like gold to me. I don't like to wander idly. I am always so relieved when I find the answer to a burning question or discover why something isn't working quite right that I want to be right. I find that a lot of our conversations these days are very revealing, and each time, I'm seeing things about her and about myself that I haven't seen before. And that is like driving to vacation in a new, beautiful city after getting lost for a few hours or minutes trying to get there. The relief of getting there overshadows the annoyances and frustrations of being lost to begin with, and the beauty of your destination makes the trip worthwhile. Your wife is a vast, often unknown country, and if your only destination is the Land of Sex, you may find your visa revoked way more often than you would like it to be. Ask for directions! Your wife and the Great God who made her know her better than anyone, so who better to ask?

Chapter 5- Emasculating the Dragon

Have you ever watched one of those Veterinarian reality shows that come on National Geographic Channel? Shows like "The Incredible Dr. Pol"? Felacia and I like to watch "Dr. Pol", but our other favorite in that genre is "Dr. Oakley, Yukon Vet." Nurses and doctors are a very unique breed of people in that they have this way of speaking about the human body and its functions in the rawest and frankest of terms. I've experienced this rawness firsthand because Felacia was a practicing nurse for 17 years. Dr. Oakley, though she doctors on animals and not humans, is no exception when it comes to that raw honesty about her work. It was from watching Dr. Oakley that I learned about the emasculator.

For a man, an emasculator might be perhaps the most nightmarish of medieval torture devices, something he'd awake from dreaming about in a cold sweat. I have seen the Good Doctor use the emasculator many times on her television show. Oftentimes, she and her assistant would corral an unruly bull at one of her client's farms out in the Yukon. They would often have to get the help of the farmer or rancher who owned the property to subdue the animal. Dr. Oakley, Sharpshooter, would use a blowgun to shoot the bull with a tranquilizer dart. Sometimes two. After fighting the effects of the drugs and stumbling about for a few minutes, the massive animal would slowly get lethargic, then gradually stagger over onto its side. It would roll to the ground in a deep sleep. Its thick tongue would loll out of the side of its mouth. Finally, when the animal was completely rendered senseless, Dr. Oakley would scramble to begin the procedure for which all the hassle was necessary: a castration.

Yes, guys, you read that right. Dr. Oakley was there to cut that poor bull's balls off. Dr. Oakley would grab the whole handful of that bull's genitals and pull them slightly until they were stretched enough to get the emasculator ready to cut just above the gonads.

That emasculator is a wicked looking device. Here is how Wikipedia describes the emasculator- "An emasculator is a tool used in the castration of livestock. Its function is to simultaneously crush and cut the spermatic cord, preventing hemorrhaging while still detaching the testis from the animal." It resembles a big set of cable cutters and serves the same basic function. Doc Oakley enslaves the testicles just beneath the steel grasp of the emasculator blades, then she forcefully presses the handles together until you hear a satisfying crunch, and the offended organs are laying in the palm of her hand. There is always a sickening crunch when she does the deed, and I always wonder if the show's producers add the sound effects to enhance the terrible finality of the whole procedure. I always cringe when I hear that crunch.

The worst thing is that Dr. Oakley so unceremoniously tosses the poor animal's manhood into the grass nearby, as if it were never there.

The emasculator: so terrible, yet so necessary! Its function, and that of the doctor who wields it, is strangely similar to that of the knight going in to that fearsome dragon. Often your hurting wife, who has become so mean and snappy and angry, has developed a tremendous need for self-protection. This may be for various reasons. She may have been raised in an abusive home as child, a home that was physically, verbally, or sexually abusive. You as a husband may have been abusive in the past, or still may be. She may have felt abandoned in some way at some point by someone.

37

She may have had one or more truly tragic or horrific experiences with men, or women perhaps. She may have been neglected in some way. Whatever her experience was, she has retreated into herself, into her cave, and she is breathing incendiary fire on anyone who tries to invade that sacred space. Often as a husband, you may still find yourself unwelcome in that sacred space because deep down, she doesn't trust you to uphold the safety she has found there.

We have all heard of marriages where it is said that the wife wears the pants in the family. This is really just another way of saying she is the dominant entity in the household. In many ways, we could say her husband has been emasculated by her. She rules the roost. The head of household has had his balls clipped, and he's a shell of a man.

One of the possibilities that a husband may discover, if he has chosen to journey into the dark regions of the dragon's lair, is that he is actually there to emasculate the dragon. The one who has been clipped may be the one who needs to do the clipping. What I said is exactly what I meant to say; the husband, the knight, is there to clip his wife's masculinity. Women in the absence of a man in the home have a remarkable ability to fulfill both the male and female roles. Even with the man in the home, if she believes he is passive or absent in any way that leaves her or her children unprotected or insecure, she will "put on the pants", so to speak. A husband who is going in to rescue his loving wife from the terrors plaguing her has to be prepared to be an emasculator. I have always believed that my feminine side is Felacia. I am her masculine side. But sometimes it's easy to forget who you are in the relationship.

Emasculating a wife is a very gentle, loving, tender operation. If you have ever heard the phrase "Kill them with kindness", you'll know how you should approach a wife who has had to become aggressive to accomplish what she needs. You're not going in to subdue and destroy. You are going to slowly and surely win her trust by being the man of your house.

I tend to be emotional at times, a bit of a dreamer and a bit of a romantic in my thinking. Felacia is matter-of-fact and very bold. I tend to be monotone and mostly quiet in speech. She is boisterous, with a ready laugh and a fiercely passionate approach to life and what she believes. She is a go-getter and tends to be self-driven. Early in our marriage, she was the one who made the wheels turn. She got our first apartment in her name. She paid for my tux, my brothers tux, and my cousins tux so we could all be dressed for the wedding. She went out and bought our first couch, with her money. She was in many ways the head of our house, even though I was present. I only spoke up about necessary things like bills or life needs if it affected me personally. Otherwise, I let her handle it. She did it all very well, but a few years in, she got really tired. She is 4 years younger than I am, but she was handling everything. She had already been in the mode that no man was going to control or take advantage of her before we got married, and after marriage, she doubled down on her aggressive need to control the world around her. It wasn't until much later, with lots of prayer and talks with her and others, that I realized she had become the way she was because she felt the need to protect herself. As she told me some things later in our marriage about why she was the way she was, my heart went out to her. I gradually felt more and more responsible to be her protector and not her attacker. When we were young in our marriage, I would often attack her verbally if I felt she was disrespecting me or being overbearing. But as I got to know her and more about her, my view of her began to change.

One of the goals of the knight going into the lair is that his usual role as protector is not for the usual reason. You as a husband are not going in to the dark places where those hurting parts of your wife reside to attack her or attack anything for her. You are as much going in as a surgeon as you are a knight. In your own way, you are there to emasculate her, to take away the masculine modes of protection she has taken on. You are going to do this by becoming the man you promised her you would be when you married her. I believe every wife wants to be a woman. Every wife is a woman, you may be thinking right now! And you're right. But she may not feel like one. If she feels unprotected by you, if she feels like she's supporting you physically or emotionally more than what she needs to, she may feel overwhelmed. She may have deep-seated, unresolved issues that are trapped in the midst of raising kids, being a wife, a career woman, and these issues remain an open wound that never get sorted through. Before you know it, you're dealing with a dragon. But when you go in to her with a genuine desire to defend, support and protect her, for her sake, it disarms her. Her fire is quenched. She is emasculated. And she is happy. You're allowing her to be the woman she really wants to be by being the man, the knight, she needs you to be. I believe the happiest homes should be the ones where the man knows who he is, and thusly he treats his wife with the care and concern she deserves. And in this process, the man also defeminizes himself.

This is the other side of the coin when a man is not being a man in his home and his marriage. He feminizes himself in unhealthy ways. Felacia, for example, is very emotional and passionate in ways that only a woman should be. At times in our marriage when I have taken on the same traits that make her uniquely female, I become pouty, whiny, and petulant, like a spoiled teenage boy. When I approach as a knight, instead of that teenage boy, she quiets down and becomes a soft, little kitten. Yes, she could claw and bite, but my care and concern disarm her aggressive need to protect herself. She knows I have become a safe place for her.

I become Dr. Oakley to her wild, bullish side, and she is docile as a fawn, because now she is allowed to be.

Chapter 6- Men are Waffles, Women are Spaghetti?

I've heard it said that men are like waffles and women are like spaghetti. Men tend to be compartmentalized in their thinking, more focused, while women seem to bounce from topic to topic, which would be considered more random and abstract. I've also heard the concept that men are from Mars and women are from Venus. The whole point of both ideas is that men and women are vastly different in the ways that they think. For many years, men and women have been prepared for marriage by counselors, pastors, parents, and friends with the idea that "the two of you are like night and day, completely different from each other in every way mentally and physically." Somehow, this preparation is supposed to be a sort of insulator for the shock of realizing how completely unlike you your spouse is after you first get married. I remember the thought pervading in my head when I was a young man in college: whoever I marry is going to be an uncharted, wild wilderness of emotions that I would have to fight to understand. As I have gotten older, I really wonder if some of our ideas about the thought patterns and emotions of men and women are actually more binding and restrictive than we realize.

Now obviously, I'm no psychologist, my brothers. I'm just an old machinist down in LA, Lower Alabama, as we say down here, but somehow, I think men and women are both a lot more complex than we are given credit for. I'd even venture to say both sexes might be like a shovelful of spaghetti piled on a couple of waffles! Here's a recent example. Last night, I was riding around the refinery where I work with my work partner. Just as a backstory, my partner is a new employee at our company, but he used to work for AT&T up north. He did some work installing fiber-optic cable and wiring for the phone system. So last night he told me that he was still having to get used to working around other people. He said he always worked by himself for the first several years at the phone company, and later when he was assigned a partner, the two of them still worked from separate trucks on completely separate city blocks. My partner is a lot like me: laidback and calm and doesn't seem to be quick-tempered. He told me he's the type of person who is quite happy and completely comfortable working all by himself, but he's also able to work with nearly anyone. I am generally known to be the same way at work, even though I think everyone there would actually be surprised at how quick-tempered I can be at times. More on that later.

When my partner said this to me, I was fascinated. But I was even more fascinated by his next statement. He said his father was completely the opposite. He told me when he was a kid, and his dad was working on something, his dad wanted him standing right there next to him, even if he was just holding a wrench in his hand. His dad wanted his company the whole time. He didn't like being by himself. That was how he was wired. I proceeded to tell my partner that Felacia is the same way. She likes to do things together, with a group, interactively. I, on the other hand, might have made a great sniper in the military because I don't mind being by myself, working on something. That trait comes in handy as a writer. Not so much as a public speaker, something Felacia is brilliant at. Anything where she is around people or interacting with people, she is brilliant. She lights up a room. But we're very opposite in this way.

Now what fascinated me about my partner and his father was this: his father's need for company was not based on his gender, but on his personality. This particular man likes community, but his son, his own flesh and blood, likes solitude. Both of them are males, but in this way, they are completely different. I know a lot of guys who are very quiet and solitary. They like to be alone. I know a lot of guys that are very boisterous and loud and fun and like to be

44

around others. I know a lot of women of both personality traits as well. There is no formula to any of it. God made us as human beings to be very complex and random, like the earth itself. I believe God put the elements we needed as humans on the earth for us to have in abundance. The trees, rocks, water, air, coal, bacteria.... every kind of animal, vegetable, mineral, or substance we might possibly need to live is here on our planet. The twist is that God didn't take all those materials and craft them into skyscrapers, cars, books, beds, or Louis Vuitton purses (Felacia would love to pick a few of those off a tree). He laid all those materials out on the earth and beneath it in some form and told mankind in Genesis 1:28, "be fruitful and increase in number; fill the earth and subdue it." Take all those elements and make what you need out of them. And He gave mankind the intelligence to figure out what to do with it all.

So what in the world does that have to do with men and women and marriage?

I believe the same way God made the earth complex and random, and with no obvious order to it (He always has an order; even beneath seeming chaos, He always makes sense), he made both men AND women complex and random at times. Sometimes, I believe both men and women are waffles. Or spaghetti. And often both at the same time. God, when He made Adam and Eve, said they would be One Flesh. This means that two very different people would eventually, in marriage, become one person, in their decisions, their goals and thoughts, and their direction. They would take the complex and random elements of themselves, their minds, and begin to assemble it into one marriage, just like a skyscraper is composed of metals and glass and concrete that was formed and shaped to create something we humans could use. If God made us to be one flesh as man and wife, wouldn't it make sense that our complexities were formed so that we could take all that "stuff" and make something useful?

Felacia told me one day that I am actually a big bowl of spaghetti. I'm a lot more emotionally driven than my calm, quiet demeanor would suggest. And she, in her fun, lively way, is more of a waffle in some ways than we thought. She can tend to be rather black and white in the way she thinks about things. I often have a lot of gray in the middle of my black and white, but between the two of us we manage to make something sensible out of it all. I would venture to say that men and women have been enslaved in a way to the idea that men think on one track: sex, football, cars, work etc. Everything is in a compartment. But even waffles have syrup that overlaps from one section to another. Men are the same way. Our human brains can connect so many disparate elements together at one time that trying to categorize our thoughts all the time can be unhealthy. As I said earlier, I'm relatively quiet and laid-back. Based on common societal ideas, I have always assumed I was not easily angered, nor did I have a bad temper, just because of my personality. Not the case at all! It wasn't until I got married that I realized how bad my temper was at times. Grouchy, mean, moody...but men don't have mood swings, do we? We just get mad sometimes. Sometimes, we get sad. Sometimes we're happy. No matter our mood, I think we are expected to shove it into a compartment. So the fact that I had an underlying sense of anger that ran in an underground stream throughout my young life on into adulthood was transformed into "Yeah, I get annoyed sometimes," or "I don't know why I got mad. I'm not like this normally...." Sadness, anger, joy, peace, confusion, so many emotions and feelings can run their course through our lives and our minds as men, and as men, we do our best to keep those emotions in their compartments. But I think acknowledging them helps us be better, more satisfied men, and husbands.

The dangerous part of this corralled way of thinking is that men are given cartoonishly effeminate traits in most portrayals that don't fit the men are waffles notion. Our American society seems to emasculate men in any way it can possibly find, from portraying men as lazy oafs who can barely put on their own shoes in the morning, to ravenous, oversexed animals who can barely keep their pants on at the sight of a woman. I truly believe men are more complex than what we are given the chance to be. The knight is there, but the drag queen is celebrated instead, and men feel lost in the middle. Somewhere, deep in the dragon's cave, many knights have taken a seat in the dark, completely lost, with no memory of why they entered the cave to begin with. And far too many are exiting the cave dressed as princesses themselves, or covering their faces in shame as news of their infidelities and ravenous sins are made public. The dragons begin to grow in number and fury. It seems that all is lost.

It is in these times, when the hobbits are content with their pipeweed and the ringwraiths are at the door of the hobbit hole, that hope can be found. A quest is calling, one that only your kind can accomplish. Gandalf waits at the door with an adventure.

Chapter 7- The quest begins

You may have noticed I'm quite a movie buff. I am not tremendously picky with what I watch as genres go, but I like action, a good story, and interesting characters. And I love stories that have some kind of a difficult quest for the characters to undertake, normally one that will require every inch of their endurance and will. The journey Frodo and Sam and their friends take to carry Sauron's Ring of Power, the one great ring, to Mount Doom in Mordor in *The Lord of the Rings* trilogy of movies are perhaps my favorite set of movies of all time. They may be the quintessential set of quest movies. There's the unqualified hero who leads the band of unlikely partners to fulfill the quest. There's the almost insurmountable villain to beat, against nearly impossible odds. There are the partners, each of whom have unique skills that are often previously honed for the task. And there is the burden that must be carried to its ultimate, final destination.

You may be thinking that marriage is the burden, but marriage is actually like Middle Earth, the realm in which the characters live. The burden may change over the years. For the people of Middle Earth in Tolkien's story, the particular burden at that particular time was one that was a running threat to their very existence for thousands of years, the Ring of Power. In the beginning, a great war averted the threat, and the Ring of Power was lost for many, many years. By the time of the first story in the Trilogy, the Ring had resurfaced, and with it the great Sauron and his vast army. The overarching threat that shadowed their realm had returned, and it was time to end the threat once and for all. Marriage can be much the same way. There can often be lingering shadows in our marriages, shadows of things from even before you married each other, that cause conflict, anger and sadness.

Let me tell you another story.

When this year began, we had several significant life events take place in our lives, all of which centered around my beloved spouse. First, Felacia had a pretty major surgery, with a seven-week recovery time. It was a sensitive surgery, and a scary one at her age, but we felt it was necessary. Secondly, at the end of the previous year, we had an unfortunate incident at the house with some of our extended family that caused a rift which has yet to be resolved in some ways. And finally, the whole of last year and on into this year, Felacia has been a stay-at-home mom. She has a bachelor's degree in nursing and was a nurse for 18 years. She's had some chastisement sent her way by well-meaning family about coming off of her job that really bothered her, since she was already ambivalent about coming home, so it's been a challenge for her. All these things were God's will for us and have been a good thing in the end. Even so, the transitions in all these events have been challenging. But a life preserver was thrown into our lives that changed everything at the time. A good friend encouraged Felacia to read a book that her book group was reading. It was called *The Emotionally Healthy Woman* by Geri Scazzero.

This book began a quest for us as a couple. I had no intention of reading the book with her, but many of the things she told me as she read got me curious. So I began to read along with her, at my own pace and on my own time. It was as if the book was a call to begin a journey into some issues that had been plaguing us since we first married. Her pastor friend was like Gandalf, calling on us to take a journey, and as we went, our fellowship of friends went with us. It was like Geri Scazzero was a companion on this quest, as we read about how she learned to overcome the need to overextend herself, to say "no" when she needed to, to speak up when she needed to. Many of the struggles she dealt with were a revelation, not only to my wife, but to me. And the resolves she found in the midst of the trials were a relief to her, who after years of serving and accommodating others, found herself in a lonely cave. I, on the other hand, was actually in one of the better places in my life and my emotions, a place of less spaghetti and more waffles, but I reached a place where I, instead of being annoyed by her emotions, wanted to walk into wherever she was hiding and walk back out together. So we completed the book together. If I could, I would rename Geri's book *The Emotionally Healthy Person*. It was as much a blessing to me as it was to Felacia. There are places you as a husband will go with your wife that you can only go together because where you're going is not just for you or for her separately, but for both of you. There may be places or times that you go to some places that your wife needs to go with you. There were a few years around the time of Hurricane Katrina that Felacia had to walk through some hard places with me. I'm from New Orleans, Louisiana originally, so Katrina in 2005 was like losing a family member. The devastation in New Orleans was devastating emotionally to many people, myself included. My dad died two weeks later, post Katrina. Then my younger brother died 3 years later in 2008 at the age of 32, hit and killed by a 17-year old drunk driver. We all go through tough periods, and for me, those years were some of the toughest. And through all of it, Felacia walked with me, through my moods and funks. We all have hard periods in our lives. But some of us have no one to walk through them with us.

This wasn't the first time I'd walked a walk with her like this. The first time, she read a book called *Every Woman's Battle* by Shannon Ethridge. That book at that time was a breakthrough in the issues both she and I were dealing with. At a very young age, I developed a problem with an unhealthy sexual lust that was driven not by physical activity but by things I saw. It had always been a secret problem, but by the time we married, I was several years into a real addiction to pornography, something I'd gotten a hold of in full in college. I got a real deliverance of a sort from it in 2001, but it was still a struggle years later. My sweet wife, my princess, now my queen, had become a dragon over time as I fought this battle with pornography, along with the myriad of other issues I dealt with as a young, selfish man. Felacia became angry at my distance, my aloofness, my lack of sex drive toward her after she found out....it was a time. So this particular book was a very needed quest for us. As she read it, I could tell she was changing. She was softening. So I began to read it with her. I began to understand some things from her perspective, and how what I was doing as a man was affecting her. The book was not written to men, but it helped me to see what she saw. That was my part of the quest.

By the time Felacia was reading *The Emotionally Healthy Woman*, I had been on many journeys with her, but often they were from issues dealing with me. She supported me through the journey, but I was the one healing. This was the first time that I felt a need to take a quest with her that had virtually nothing to do with anything I had done wrong. It wasn't to fix me or anything I had done. It was a quest purely for her, for things she needed resolve in. So we had a chance to spend the last year together. She is no longer passing me as I passed her, headed in from work or out to work. She is home full time, and I work one week on, one week off. It was as if God said, "Okay, Joel, we've dealt with you all these years, and she's hung in there with you. Now it's her turn." It's like He gave us a chance to really become one for a year, then He put us in a position to begin to take her quest, which was our quest. I could recall many times in the past, when we would argue, and she would say that she wished we could finally get my issues dealt with so we could spend some time dealing with her emotional needs. The time had finally come!

Now, I am by no means saying I have dealt with all my issues, but God had gotten us to a point that now she felt safe enough to let me walk into the cave with her. The fellowship was truly a fellowship this time, a walk together to win the day, not a walk of shame like so many others when I went in to the dragon. I used to always feel like I was apologizing for something as I approached Felacia during those times in her cave of despair, my shield up, her fire blazing. It wasn't a quest so much as a penance. Every time before that, I had to wear armor, heading in to face a dragon. But this time was a lot different. It really felt like we walked in together, hand in hand, to face the things that awaited us.

Chapter 8- Greener Grass?

A few years ago, we bought a late model Infiniti SUV. We had given away our faithful 2004 Tahoe for an upgrade to the pinnacle of luxury and the chance to get away from some of the small issues the Tahoe was having. I loved that Tahoe as much as a human can love an inanimate object. I was always bragging that I hadn't found anything that its cargo area wasn't big enough to hold, that we had taken trips all over the country, and that it rarely put us down. It was a great vehicle, and as of this writing, it is still on the road with its new owners. The Infiniti we have now is a gorgeous vehicle. It's got sumptuous black leather (yes, I meant to say sumptuous), smooth, classic lines, and the most unique color that that particular model comes in....it is a beauty.

Let me begin by saying, Felacia and I have never owned a vehicle that has had to go to the dealer's repair shop as many times as our Infiniti! Now in its defense, it was used and had had two previous owners before us. One or both of those owners dogged it out pretty badly by the time we got it. Our most major repair was replacing the transmission about a month or so after we bought it. That was a $14,000 repair which by God's grace was covered under our warranty. We also replaced the catalytic converter. We replaced the navigation/climate control computer, which crashed when I tried to update it with faulty update disks the maker sent to me. We replaced all the ignition coils and spark plugs. Our old Tahoe was looking better and better, and I began to regret giving it away. Finally, we had a check engine light come on (again!) this past Sunday, so I applied for a car loan, and we went car shopping.

We looked at several Tahoes and GMC Yukons, most newer than our Infiniti. They were all nice, but in the end, we just couldn't do it. We owed so little on what we have, and we've put so much into it. We had more than enough car loan to buy something else, and it was merely a matter of deciding what to buy before we left the dealer with a new car. But it just didn't make sense, with all the work we had done to our Infiniti and how little we owed, to get into another car note. We genuinely like our Infiniti. It drives so smoothly, it's comfortable, and it still looks great when you walk up to it in the parking lot. Sure, it has a few scratches on close inspection, but it's a very nice ride.

The grass may seem greener on the other side, but it still has to be mowed. I think as men, we can often see our wives as the Mrs. and I were seeing our vehicles. Sometimes you see the woman wearing the wedding ring you gave her like we saw our Tahoe: strong and reliable, but well-worn and soon to be in the need for some repairs and updates. Sometimes you see her like we saw our Infiniti: beautiful and appealing, but very high maintenance and more work than you are ultimately willing to put in. And sometimes you see her as we recently saw our Infiniti: needing to be replaced for something easier and cheaper to maintain. Even though we realized that we really liked what we had, and we'd like to continue to maintain it and continue to invest in keeping it nice, we had a hard decision to make. There was no one to decide for us, no one to cautiously ask us "Hey, do you really want to get into another note, and a purchase that will ultimately leave you owing more than you currently owe for what you have?" In the long run, had we made a purchase, we would have been less satisfied. Everything we drove at the dealership that day seemed like a step down from what we already owned, and we had already done so much to repair it and make it nice. You may find that you get frustrated with your wife, and you think about trading her in on a newer, younger model. Maybe you think she complains a lot. Maybe you think she's high-maintenance. Maybe you are unhappy with her weight gain or areas that you think have physically changed over the years. Maybe you just have a history with women and a wandering eye. Or perhaps you have been a cheater in the past or present.

Marriage and love are daily, sometimes hourly choices that all married people make. It is a mature decision made by adults. In our microwave age, we as humans seem to be more and more driven by ease and less willing to wait on things to mature, to grow. In our own immaturity, we aren't willing to let things and people around us mature either. If we don't see instant results, we're ready to lay it all down and go back into debt, just because it's easy. Just as your wife has changed over the years, so have you. It is 99.9% likely that she sees things that might make her think about trading you in just as much as you may think about trading her in. The problem is that all relationships will take work. I realized in my attempt to purchase another car, I was making the same mistake I've made many times over the years. It seems easier to get something new than to work with what you have. My beautiful wife is comparable to a Bentley or a Rolls Royce, but she's always been a challenge for me. She requires me to work at being a good husband. I don't always do a good job. There have been times in the past that I was ready to trade her in for a Yugo, just because it was easier. But I realize how God has blessed me with the best woman in the world, and He has given me the privilege of trying my best to be the best man for her. I fail miserably at times, but I eventually succeed because I keep trying. I'm not going to quit. I'm going to get better at it. I love her very much, and I want to win the queen's heart again and again. It does seem like a daunting task at times, because I am truly not an expert, but with God on my side, I'm up to the task. If you're a man, you're up to the task too. I believe God has made one of our greatest accomplishments as men to be winning the hand of our wives. Truly winning her hand is not just saying "I do", but loving her as Christ loved the church, wherein we lay our lives down for our wives.

I know there have been many times that Felacia has wanted to trade me in. I am very high-maintenance in my own way, and she has to grit her teeth with me constantly. In many ways she has laid down her life for me and our family, because she loves God, if nothing else. Laying down your life is a mutual thing between a husband and a wife. It's much like laying down the opportunity to trade out into another car. The choice is always there, but somehow, the choice seems far less appealing when true maturity sets in. The young Joel would have left that dealership with another car, just because I could have, and I had the finances approved. But the maturing Joel left with a better vehicle than anything we test drove, because we put the work in to make it that way.

I am largely responsible for the beautiful woman I wake up to in the morning. I am largely responsible for the dragon I wake up to as well. Either way, it's what I see in her and what I put into her. If you are not seeing the wife you expected to see after all these years, evaluate what you have been investing in her. This is something she will have to do as well, if she feels you are not the man she expects you to be. The Bible says "We reap what we sow." I can't sow rocks and expect roses. Yet somehow we often do, or we look over in our neighbor's yard and admire the grass in his garden.

Again, the grass looks greener on the other side, but it still has to be mowed. Marriage takes work, but the rewards are great! Proverbs 5:15-21 in the New International Version says "Drink water from your own cistern, running water from your own well. Should your springs overflow in the streets, your streams of water in the public squares? Let them be yours alone, never to be shared with strangers. May your fountain be blessed, and may you rejoice in the wife of your youth. A loving doe, a graceful deer- may her breasts satisfy you always, may you ever be intoxicated with her love. Why, my son, be intoxicated with another man's wife? Why embrace the bosom of a wayward woman? For your ways are in full view of the LORD, and he examines all your paths". In other words, enjoy the riches to be found in the wife of your youth, that beautiful woman you married. Whether you think she is or not, she's still there. For many years, I forgot that the gorgeous girl I married was still there, until I began to drink water from my own cistern. I only saw the dragon in the cave, blowing fire at me when I approached. But as time passes, Felacia gets more and more lovely. She is no less work, for sure. Let me be clear on that! But I am more determined to do the work to see my diamond shine again. I am having to mature to match the woman that I am married to now versus the young girl I exchanged vows with. That is the great adventure that awaits all married men who choose it.

Chapter 9- The "F" Bomb

Has your wife ever dropped an "F" bomb on you? Now, I'm not talking about the "F" bomb we all know and don't love. I'm talking about the one called "Feelings". As in she wants to talk about her feelings. As in she wants to know how you're feeling about not getting that promotion. As in the Man of Steel must still somehow, somewhere, have a heart way down deep inside that no one is allowed to see.

"Feelings" can be a bad word to a man in a relationship with a woman, a word that takes him into the cave of the dragon in ways that he never imagined and never wanted to go in the first place. As boys, we are often taught that crying is soft, emotions are weak, and communicating those "feelings" is a practice that dwells in the realm of the female. We are taught in our society that women are almost natural born experts in the realm of emotion and feelings, and we as a society have all drunk the kool-aid so to speak in believing that this is true. We are given the impression that men are emotionally crippled from birth, and remain that way until death, and women have an almost guru-like grasp of how they feel and why. That's what we are told without being told, and we all tend to accept it as fact. I'm no psychologist or psychiatrist, but I believe that this is a harmful lie that has been perpetuated for eons. I think it is often a fear of entering the realm of feelings that strikes terror into the knight who even remotely considers entering the cave to retrieve his princess.

I can remember when we were young married, and Felacia would corner me on one of our rare date nights. We spent perhaps the first 10 or more years working a schedule where I worked day shift during the week and she worked night shift on the weekend. It seemed like we were always passing the kids off like a relay race, and our time together was rare. And when we finally did get time together, she wanted to talk about "us". This meant we needed to hash out all the unresolved emotional things that we never got to sit down and talk about because we were always busy. I hated those talks. I used to complain that we ruined the little time that we had to enjoy being together by talking about our differences of opinion, but in reality, looking her in the eye and talking about how I felt scared me. Talking about how she felt scared me even more, because I felt like she was always mad at me about something. So I dreaded date night.

As the years have passed, I have learned that talking through things is one of the greatest practices to aid in a successful marriage. I realized that I have a lot of thoughts and feelings about a lot of things, and as a man, it is imperative that I express them. I've never been a man who talked a lot or was very expressive, so I never believed I had feelings about a lot of issues. The truth is, all men feel, from the quietest man to the most expressive. Women don't have a corner on the feelings market, and I think the average man would be quite surprised to know that many women have no earthly idea how they feel about a lot of things a lot of the time. Oftentimes for a wife, the retreat into her dragon's lair is a result of not knowing how to sort out her feelings, and coping with the fact that she feels like no one understands, especially you. The more I sit and talk with Felacia, the more I understand her. And the surprising thing is, the more I sit and talk to her, the more I understand myself. God said a man and his wife would be one flesh for a reason, and in talking to each other, you both begin to discover who you are.

Remember a few chapters back when I said I was a lot more spaghetti than I thought? I never knew that until Felacia and I sat and talked. I've always thought I was very compartmental but I'm not. My feelings change and swing as much as hers do. I feel deeply, but as men should, I try to channel those feelings into a healthy forward motion. I believe God made men and women to operate on some level of feeling, but the drive behind their feelings come from different places.

Chapter 10- #ChivalryToo

My all-time favorite scene of any movie that I have ever seen is from the Stanley Kubric film *Spartacus*. Spartacus might be one of my all-time favorite MAN movies. Man Movies are any movies where there is blood, fighting, swords, guns, cars, military equipment, intrigue, sports, and beautiful women... anything that sparks the adrenaline and sense of adventure and power in a man. These are films that appeal to a man's core values of leading the charge, righting wrongs, fixing problems, solving mysteries, saving the damsel and the day. Man Movies call on the Adam in all of us. Some Man Movies have an Eve, a beautiful woman to be rescued. Some have no Eve, and the damsel to save is the adventure itself. But it is the love between Spartacus and Varinia that that ends up rescuing them both.

As the film begins, Spartacus is a Thracian slave back during the time of the Roman empire who becomes a gladiator in the gladiatorial school of Lentulus Batiatus. The movie starts with Spartacus working in a mining pit. It is a hot, sweltering place, almost like the bowels of Hell itself, and we find Spartacus laboring amongst the other miserable slaves, breaking rocks and carrying them in heavy loads on their backs. As Spartacus carries his load, he sees one of the guards attack an old slave who is too weak to carry the huge sack of rocks. The guard begins beating the slave to motivate him, so Spartacus attacks him and "hamstrings" him. Basically, he bites the man's hamstring IN HALF!!!! Spartacus was a bad dude! We quickly see that even though Spartacus is a slave, he is ferociously clutching hold of his dignity as a man. His heart is the heart of a free man. In the course of events, Batiatus buys Spartacus, sensing his propensity to be an asset in the arena, with the aim that he can tame his animal instincts into those of a fierce gladiator. He takes Spartacus to the school, where Marcellus, an ex-gladiator himself, trains the slaves while dangling a very faint hope before them that they can survive long enough to possibly win their own freedom.

Spartacus is defiant from the start, his iron will set against Marcellus at every turn. Marcellus tries every way he can to break Spartacus, which leads to my favorite scene. It is nighttime, and Spartacus is sitting in his cell when there is a knock at the door. A guard has brought him a reward for the night: a beautiful slave girl named Varinia. One of the rewards the gladiators get is the company of a slave woman when the trainers see fit. This in itself is interesting because the gladiators are slaves who serve the needs of the wealthy patrons who come to see them battle each other. The female slaves are even further down the sordid hierarchy of the have-nots: they serve the men who serve the privileged. Servants work alongside each other; Slaves work in stacks atop each other, like oppressed blocks in a pyramid. Oftentimes, oppressed men still rule over the women who are unfortunate enough to be under their power, and this can give even a man who feels powerless a measure of the feeling that he still has power over someone in some capacity. Power in the hands of the powerless can be a dangerous thing.

So Varinia is introduced into Spartacus' small, dark, dirty cell. Varinia is Beautiful, and Spartacus is enraptured. We get the sense that he has never been with or even touched a woman before. Varinia knows the drill, so she lowers her clothes. Spartacus sees her in all her glory. I think if some women knew how the eyes of a man are ignited by the sight of a naked woman, they would be more careful about how they presented themselves. I think if some men could see the fearsome lust in their eyes when they see an attractive woman, even fully clothed, they would be far more careful with how they look at and approach a woman. I can imagine that look in a man's eyes could inspire terror in a woman's heart.

Spartacus is careful and gentle however. He approaches Varinia and caresses her shoulder and carefully inspects her. You can see that Varinia lets him do this because she has to, but she has that same defiant look in her eyes as he has in the presence of Marcellus, the look of a person who is clinging to their dignity like a life raft in the middle of the ocean, daring you to knock them off of it. As Spartacus is looking at her, he realizes that Marcellus and another guard are above them, looking down into the cell. They know he is aware of them and they begin to laugh. Spartacus steps back and screams in fury.

"I am not an Animal!!!!"

Varinia looks at him and very quietly says, "Neither am I".

Mic Drop! Literally Mic drop!

Spartacus is completely disarmed. He bends down and hands her her clothes, then begins to talk to her. He finds out who she is, and that she has been a slave since the age of thirteen. As Spartacus talks to Varinia, she stops being an object in his eyes, and becomes a fellow human being. When Spartacus gives Varinia her clothes, he disarms her, returning her value as a human being to her like a gift, and shows her a kindness she has never seen before. And he is returning his value to himself, even in humiliation.

This scene is my all-time favorite because I think this is the essence of what makes us men. It shows us what we should be. We are not animals, and neither are the women around us. Our American bent is often driven to animalize us away from our humanness, and thus our humaneness. I have been shocked since the #MeToo movement began at some of the stories I've heard about men in positions of power, and the things they would say and do and expect of the women (and the men) under their care. CEOs of entertainment companies, Tech Giants, Megachurch pastors, even political figures.... All Abusers at the highest level. I think when we abuse ourselves in any way, it is because we feel powerless. But when we abuse others, it is because it makes us feel powerful. I think there is a truer, untapped power in the ability to tame the wild animal instincts we have at times, channeling the wild man inside us and bending his will to our own will. Tarzan becomes the Earl of Greystoke, but inside the Earl of Greystoke remains the wild, fearless King of the Jungle. The appeal of Superman is that he is cloaked in a persona of a mild-mannered reporter named Clark Kent. Jesus the Son of God is cloaked in the persona of a young Jewish carpenter. And the wild man of battle is cloaked in the knight, travelling to save his princess.

As men, we are always looking for something to conquer and something to fix. I think that when we approach our wives as people that we seek to serve, to know, and not to conquer, to understand and not fix, we find in the journey that sense of adventure that every man seeks. If we as men could approach women as Jesus did on earth, with the thoughts and eyes He had, the #MeToo movement would never have come into existence. It would never have been necessary. Jesus knew that the dragon in the cave was hiding for a reason, but He also knew he was sent to seek and save that which was lost. Jesus saw the woman caught in adultery, laying in the dirt, surrounded by men ready to stone her to death and stood there as her shield from their indignation. Spartacus became a shield to Varinia. I became a shield to Felacia instead of being shielded from her. Where Adam threw Eve under the bus, Jesus instead pulled her up out of the mud, dusted her off and healed her wounded soul. It is in the ability to wound and to hurt but choosing not to do so that true power is found. The beauty of a garden is that you never go into it with the intent of plucking out every brilliant flower in it. You stay your power to enjoy the integrity of what you are seeing. The world is a garden, and the women in your life are the roses. There are a million Varinias who are innocent victims trying to live life in a world where they lack power, these young flowers being pulled out by the roots, many at very young ages. And this is where we as the knights must come in and shine. Chivalry may not be cool, but it's necessary. We are not animals, guys, despite what evolutionary theory tells us, and neither is she, whoever the particular "she" around you may be.

Now none of these admonitions excuse the fact that there have been times when women, and even our wives, have used womanhood as a weapon. Modern feminism has led some women to exploit themselves in the guise of sexual freedom, defiantly daring a man to touch them while exposing and exploiting themselves as a "protest" in some form or another. As men, it can be frustrating to see a woman dressed in a revealing way while calling you a pervert or deviant if you look at her the wrong way. This is the very height of hypocrisy. Jesus, as he dealt with the adulterous woman, knew that somewhere, perhaps even amongst the men surrounding her with stones in their hands, was an adulterous man who had been with this woman. Those accusers were hypocrites as well. Why stone the woman but not stone the man she had been laying with? Yes, hypocrisy is all around us, but it should never be an excuse for us as men not to be men, in the very best sense of the word.

Boys will be boys, as they say. They will throw stones when they are glass houses themselves. They will crucify the innocent to cover for the guilty. They will abuse and even kill the weak to entertain the wealthy and powerful. Yes, boys will be boys.

But men will be men.

Let's separate the men from the boys. Let's draw the knight out of the peasant. There are many women who were once girls, who left an innocence behind in the dirt, an innocence that someone stole from them, leaving some with the self-destructive shell that we often find amongst the abused, who are waiting for the knight to take their outstretched hand. The cave is dark where the dragon lay, the ground is hard where the woman lay, but the grip is firm and sure as you help her up. And if you are a man who has once been a boy who experienced abuse himself, you can find that man of courage in the bravery to be as Christ was, to be better, to lift a woman from the dirt, to hand a fellow slave her meager clothing, to show your wife some mercy when she's having a day.... Or a memory.

Memories can color a child's life on into adulthood for the rest of his or her life, good or bad. My dad James was molested by a male babysitter at the age of 5. That abuse tinged his whole life and our lives as his family. From the years I can remember, my mom and my dad were Christians, and they raised me, my brother, and my sister in Christ. Mom and Dad sang together (Dad studied to be an opera singer in school and Mom had a beautiful singing voice as well), and they were music ministers over the years in several churches. Yet throughout the years, I can remember times when my Dad would have an unrest in his soul and he would leave my mom for hours. It wasn't until later in my adult years that mom revealed that he would go to gay bars at some of those times. The things he experienced as a child colored his world. And they colored Mom's world as a result. And finally they colored our world as his children.

I can remember when I was a teenager, Dad found a support group of people who had gone through similar things as he had gone through. I recall him sitting us kids down and telling us what happened to him. He wasn't explicit, but he let us know it happened. So many things made sense to me then, just things about him that I noticed, little mannerisms and other things that caught my attention over the years. I was actually relieved, and very proud of him. I was really proud of Mom for riding through those things with him. It's hard to hang in there with a hurting person when they are hurting you too along the way. Mom had to have wondered how long it would take before she was forced to leave Dad to his fate. I think as a young man, a young Christian, it gave me a bit of resolve to want to be better as a man.

Pornography had gotten its tentacles around me already by that point, but I do believe God helped me then to draw a line in the sand. The part about drawing a line in the sand that we forget is that the tide will wash it away. So you have to draw it again. And again. And again. You may never stop drawing it because the tide is not a lack of resolve so much as a changing of the days. The Bible says the mercies of God are new every morning. Why? Because we need them every morning. I can remember mornings waking up, after watching porn most of the night like a zombie, feeling like I needed to be struck down by the lightning wrath of God, but somehow feeling His strange, undeserved love anyhow. And it called on the man in me, the knight, the man of chivalry, as if to say, "You screwed up, again, but it's a new day. Don't screw this one up." The tide had washed away the day before, and the sand was fresh, waiting for a new line to be drawn.

I don't know if my Dad drew a line in the sand when he got up with all those other victims of abuse and released himself from its grip, but I did. I drew a line for me. I lost the line many times.

Some days I didn't draw one. But today, all these years later, I'm still drawing that line in the sand, but seeing it far more clearly than ever. We have to go into those dark caves with each other as husbands and wives, as friends and family. The dark ones, the sad and painful ones, need a line drawn at their entrances, never to be entered again. I have drawn a line in front of pornography. I have to draw it every day. My brother, what line do you need to draw for the sake of yourself and your family? Whatever line you need to draw, resolve to do it. When we have no boundaries, abuse happens and pain is left in its wake.

I believe there's a bit of Spartacus in all of us as men, men who can learn to draw the line before ogling a woman, or rape, or adultery, or physical abuse, or sexual abuse. I believe grown men can see little girls and teenage girls as what they are, children, to protect and not abuse. I believe men who struggle with homosexual lust can still be chaste and not approach boys as my Dad's abuser did. I believe we can be better men, as Christ was, who shield women from their accusers while being men that women cannot in good conscience accuse. I believe we can be knights, who hand the thin robes of security back to our Varinias, as protectors of their virtue. I believe we are men that can draw a line, and only cross lines that God has made to be crossed.

Do you believe this is possible, men of chivalry? You do?

Me Too.

Chapter 11- Escapism vs. Enjoyment

I have heard it said of Sir Winston Churchill that he was a great leader in times of war but a poor leader in times of peace. This could be said of many of us as men. How often is a man celebrated for his accomplishments in his professional life, his achievements in the things he has created, or the intellectual pursuits he has successfully conquered, only to have failed in his personal life? There is an infamous list of the famous whose star has fallen like a meteor in life, while some of the celebrated were revealed after death to have been loathsome people on a personal level.

I have watched with great sadness the fall of the once great Bill Cosby. I mention Bill Cosby because he was one of the few of the fallen that I personally admired. I held great respect for the image he held as an exemplary father on television and off. I was never impressed with Harvey Weinstein, or Bill Clinton, or even Mr. Jobs, though I had great respect for what they accomplished. But Bill was a beacon of hope for a young black kid like me, who didn't have the sad story of some kids of my time. My home was a Christian home. Both my parents were in the home. They loved us and were good parents. I had a relatively uneventful childhood. This sort of upbringing didn't always fit the narrative for a black kid. It wasn't until I got older that I found out that there were a lot of other black kids like me that didn't grow up in single mom-led homes or in the "hood" per se. I'm definitely not saying this as a greater than-less than. My upbringing had its own set of challenges to overcome. It just means black people are as diverse as any other race of people, and black families are as diverse as other families. But it wasn't until "The Cosby Show" that I became really proud of growing up as I did. It meant our family wasn't an anomaly.

I can remember hearing people say that the Huxtable family wasn't realistic, and I always wondered why they thought so, but I would cast that off when I thought about my family and other black families we knew, who tried their best to raise their brood well. And the Huxtables helped me to realize that the Evans family on "Good Times" wasn't a bad family either, even though they had a different set of circumstances. God made us as humans to be very complex and wonderful.

Sometimes in our complexity we can succeed greatly in one area, while failing miserably in another. Great knights can make lousy kings. And great comedians can make lousy men. Cliff Huxtable unfortunately wasn't Bill Cosby. David the giant killer wasn't always David the king. David of Israel was a great knight who often made a lousy king. David was a man of many exploits, having killed the great Goliath, cutting his head off with Goliath's own sword. David and his armies conquered many of the lands and kingdoms around him, and his mighty men were men of renown, often killing armies of hundreds singlehandedly. David was an accomplished writer and musician, having written one of the greatest works of poetry ever in the book of Psalms. He was the father of the wisest king ever, King Solomon. Yet David was also known for some tremendously sad moral and political failures.

The bulk of his failures as recorded in the Bible happened in times of relative peace. One of his greatest failures was when he stole Bathsheba from her husband, eventually sinking low enough to have the man killed to cover the crime. While David's men, including Uriah, the husband of Bathsheba, were out fighting on his behalf, David was comfortable and successful enough to stay at the palace while the warriors were away. He saw Bathsheba bathing from his rooftop, was smitten with her, and sent for her right away. He slept with her and she became pregnant. Uriah was doing what

74

men are supposed to do: make it happen. David was doing what successful men sometimes do after their success: rest on their laurels. Again, David's fall was in a time of relative peace.

As men, we can often reach a level of success in our public lives that leads to a comfortable private life. We make a good living. Nice house. Nice cars. Accolades. Attention. We get bored with the success. We become proud and feel we deserve a reward. And in a sense, our success becomes a bit of a prison. Escapism slowly becomes the rule of the day as we get bored with the armor-polishing business and the restrictions of being a king. We're not Bill Cosby the up-and-coming comedian; We are William H. Cosby the successful one, and the world is wide open. It is easy to lose oneself in a world without boundaries, especially one of great success. Somehow, a man who is succeeding at home with his wife and family seems to never get lost in the wilds of his accomplishments. He always has a place to lay his head after conquering it all, a home base to ground all his accomplishments in. I believe this is the perfect will of God for man. He always wanted Adam to till the Garden of Eden with Eve at his side and their children in tow. Man and woman, we anchor each other, and Jesus is the ground we anchor in. Many great men rise to the occasion, but their knees buckle in the end, when the crisis is over and the clapping stops. They get lost in their own success and try to escape in sometimes ugly ways. Meanness. Adultery. Substance abuse. Workaholism. We begin to own our vices.

That is a difference I see in men and women. Men like to own things. I work with guys who love to hunt. And so they love guns. Now these guys are just regular old American working-class men who hunt and fish and like the outdoors. They go to the hunting camp on their two weeks off. Some of them own 30 and 40 rifles of all kinds and calibers, not to mention the pistols. These men aren't Unabombers or serial killers, just guys who like buying different guns just to own them. Some of the same guys have a car fetish. Or a fishing pole fetish. A man is proud of his pocketknife.... or his gaming laptop. These are the ways of men.

Women, however, can be a little different. They aren't into owning things so much as they like to belong to something, to be a part of something. Perhaps this is why they seem to have more of a sense of loyalty in certain ways. At one time, women were known to go to the bathroom to freshen up in groups. They seem to conduct friendships in a different way than men. They don't possess their clothes so much as they inhabit them. This sense of belonging can lead them to some of the same pitfalls that men fall into for different reasons.

I read that for all Bill Cosby's infidelities, his wife Camille was faithful to stay with him to a fault, even to the point of enabling some of his behaviors. I have heard similar commentary about Hillary Clinton, and other women in the media spotlight whose husbands have strayed. Somehow, I think this need to belong becomes warped into a loyalty to someone who is extremely disloyal in return. The unfaithful man is a master escape artist, always looking for that next fix, the next land to conquer, while his family languishes under his lack of care. And an enabling wife is like the magician's assistant, standing next to the crate as Houdini wrestles with his chains. Many men have referred to their wives as the ol' ball and chain for a reason. As I recall, the ball and chain was attached to a prisoner's ankle so that it was impossible for him to run away, and in fact made it difficult for him to even walk. It was something that any sane human would want to be free of. I would even venture to say that a woman's sense of loyalty, if cultivated properly, can be very imprisoning to an undisciplined man. But an undemanding woman can be a false heaven to such a man, because she lets him have his cake and eat it too!

Escapism is dangerous for a man. It is dangerous for his wife and his children. It allows him to hide away either in his successes or his failures, even hiding in his own sort of cave, but like Gollum clutching a Precious ring instead of a dragon blowing smoke while hoping for a rescuer. Escape artists can hide for years, until one day, their forays into darkness catch up to them, and it is discovered that what they owned was actually stolen. Another man's wife. A child's innocence. The life of another person while the escape artist drives drunk.

Enjoyment, however, is exhilarating! A man enjoys what he enjoys, but he is able to add it to the collection of wonderful things in his life. This is the glory of a true collector. Here's an example. I like to play video games on my PS4. But instead of playing for hours on end as a form of escape as I used to do, now I play for fun, when I get a chance and feel like playing. I used to feel bad about playing because I overdid it, but now playing is a part of the collection of fun things I get to enjoy in life, along with dinner with Felacia, SEX, doing projects on the house, listening to a good podcast... I feel like my life is a collection of things to enjoy instead of a stash of guilty pleasures to hide away. I am learning to own my joy instead of leasing it from someone else, even if that someone else is my wife.

There is a majesty when a man takes ownership, especially of his family. He loves his wife. He raises his sons. He teaches his daughters. He serves God. He indulges and collects joy, wherever it can be honorably found. Nothing is stolen, but all is given and received willingly. No one is a prisoner, so no one seeks to escape. A great king is a servant, not a slave, so he does everything he does because he chooses to do it. He is loyal to his people even as they are loyal to him.

Great knights can become great kings. But only if they realize that war is a temporary, necessary evil. Kings are measured by the peace of their kingdoms. Successful comedians, doctors, presidents, pastors...all are measured by the integrity of their lives over the whole span of how they lived them. Famous can become infamous in an instant. The warrior puts down the sword when the war is won. He owns the victory and cultivates the spoils. The husband puts away the wandering eyes and hands when he marries, satisfying all with his wife. And a great man doesn't hide behind success to excuse failure.

If you as man enjoy fishing, or reading, or going to car shows, or college football games, enjoy it. Own it! Have a shelf of things in your life that you indulge in and enjoy, while including your wife in the parts where she fits in that equation. In a healthy marriage, I believe both spouses can have things they enjoy together and apart, while their kingdom remains healthy. A king enjoys his kingdom when he has worked to make it secure.

This is the measure of a man.

Chapter 12- Learning to Be Loyal

There are a few things about a king that separate him from a knight or a prince.

A king has borders to his kingdom. He doesn't leave his borders to fight battles; his army does. A king rules in his domain. And a king is loyal to his subjects.

None of these criteria are in the scope of a knight. A knight leaves the borders of the kingdom at the king's command. A knight doesn't rule; he does what he's told to do. A knight is loyal because he is paid to be loyal. And a knight keeps his position by fighting. When I first married Felacia, I had to become a skillful knight because we fought a lot. I was king over myself, but when I got married, there was an element of kingship and responsibility over a new family that was very daunting to me. I remember when we were first married, I was working at a biomedical library at a local college in our town. Felacia, who is 4 years younger than me, was a new nurse, an RN, making a really good salary. I was so immature at 26, so she took the reins as best she could, fearfully but boldly as a young wife, trying to make our lives and our marriage work. I went to my low paying job, then came home. That was the extent of what I felt responsible for. A lot of times she cooked dinner, worked a 12 hour shift at the hospital, two days off three on, three off two on, left the job at 6 in the morning on payday Fridays to run around for several hours paying bills...only to come home to a husband who more often than not had gone to the local X-rated movie store the night before to buy some porno movie to throw in the trash bin before she came home. These were the days before smartphones and easy access to such things, and I was the poor excuse for a king that she was coming home to.

I was a poor knight as well. I was leaving the borders of our marriage for pornography, fighting for a selfish tyrant instead of a husband. I definitely wasn't ruling over anything. My selfishness and immaturity were overrunning our borders and wreaking havoc on the land. And any loyalty I had was because I was being paid to be loyal, as a knight would, and not a king. I was loyal in the way that an owner is loyal, but not loyal in the way a lover is loyal. My kingdom was falling apart. My poor young wife cried a lot. She was angry a lot. She became hard. I knew why, but I didn't know why. I was like a kid who is being chastised for spilling his milk on the floor because he wasn't paying attention. I thought I was in trouble for spilling the milk when the issue was that I wasn't paying attention. I thought I was in trouble for the pornography, when the real issue was the selfish nature, the immaturity that led to the symptoms. As men we often get lost in the act but neglect the cause, so the act resurfaces, and we find ourselves repenting to our wives about the same acts over and over again. It's not the action, guys, it's the heart. When the heart changes, the action will change. It may take time, but it will change.

I can remember when I had a real change of heart in regards to our marriage. We married in November of 1999. On September 11, 2001, my sweet wife was coming home that morning from yet another night shift. The night before I had spent yet another night watching something porn-related, and was laying in bed dreading the possibility that she'd suspect by my strange demeanor what I had been doing....again. My sister called that morning and asked if I had seen the news about the plane hitting one of the twin towers in New York. I was shocked, so I turned on the television. As I watched, a second plane hit the second tower. I was flabbergasted!

Many of us remember that horrible day, but one thing it marked for me was the fact that so many people died that day. People die every day, in horrible ways. And here I was mired in something so petty as Porno Movies! It was a wake-up call.

I would love to tell you that that was the last day I watched anything porn-related, but I'd be lying. While 9/11 was a turning point, my wake-up call was that PEOPLE, that great generality, were being hurt. Not my person, my wife, but people. A care and concern for the general population may still not translate into a care and concern for YOUR wife. That kind of care is in the realm of kings. But I will say that from the knight a prince was born that day.

What's the difference between Me the knight and Me the prince? Once again, a knight fights, a prince learns. A prince is learning that he will be a king one day and will be responsible for the subjects under his care. A prince is learning to be a ruler. So the realization that I was responsible for someone other than myself was a transition from knight to prince. A knight is responsible to someone; kings are responsible for someone. And princes are learning that responsibility. Princes are learning to be loyal, as kings are. My years as a prince were many! I would say about 17 years in fact. At many points in those years I struggled with pornography, selfishness, aloofness, weariness, frustration with the hardness I saw in Felacia. Many struggles! And she wasn't perfect either during those years, so I was also learning to be a imperfect king over an imperfect queen. Who was sometimes a dragon!

I believe what makes a good king is his loyalty to his subjects. Everything he does should be in the interests of securing and expanding his kingdom, making it better and greater over the years. I can say with time that I have definitely transitioned from being a knight to a prince by learning loyalty. When the wife and I argue, I don't hack and slash at her as if she's wearing armor too. Queens and princesses don't wear armor, guys, so when you argue or disagree, don't fight her like a man, verbally or physically. The softness and beauty you loved about her when you married her is maintained by you. Nobody else. If she's become a hard, scaly dragon, you need to evaluate what you've been doing or not doing. And if she's been a hard dragon, and she suddenly becomes soft and sweet, maybe you are doing something right. If so, find out what it is if you don't know already, and keep it up!

I believe women are innately loyal, and they have to be trained to be disloyal. I believe men have to be trained to be loyal. How often have you seen an abused woman stay with an abusive man, and have to be convinced to leave him? A man who doesn't abuse, who doesn't hack and slash, is a man who knows why he does what he does, and so he is loyal in what he does. I know I love Felacia, and that colors how I treat her more and more. And with that knowing grows loyalty. As loyalty grows, the prince becomes the king.

And dragons turn into queens.